A Pocke

the

A Pocket Guide to
the Bible

Scott
Hahn

Our Sunday Visitor Publishing Division
Our Sunday Visitor, Inc.
Huntington, Indiana 46750

Copyright © 2008 by Our Sunday Visitor Publishing Division, Our Sunday Visitor, Inc. Published 2008

11 10 09 08   1 2 3 4 5 6 7 8 9

Our Sunday Visitor Publishing Division
Our Sunday Visitor, Inc.
200 Noll Plaza
Huntington, IN 46750

ISBN: 978-1-59276-443-3 (Inventory No. T680)
LCCN: 2008923975

Cover design by Amanda Miller
Cover photo: Finsiel/Alinari/Art Resource, NY
Interior design by Monica Haneline

PRINTED IN THE UNITED STATES OF AMERICA

Table of Contents

Introduction

God has spoken to us "in many and various ways" (Heb 1:1). He speaks to us in the wonders of creation; for he made all the universe through his eternal Word (Jn 1:3). He speaks to us in the written story of creation and salvation that we find in the Bible — in the law, prophets, Gospel, and Apostles.

Yet all these various strains harmonize perfectly in the person of the Word made flesh, Jesus Christ. In Jesus, God communicated himself completely. Yet even then he spoke to us in words. Jesus spoke, preached, counseled, taught, and prayed aloud. He asked questions. He told stories. He even traced words in the sand. He did all of this for our sake, because words are a normal human thing. Nevertheless, his words are extraordinary, because they are revelatory. They are human words that reveal the eternal Word of God. They are the Word of God in the words of men and women and children.

In the Bible, we encounter not a dead letter, but a person: the "Word of God . . . living and active" (Heb 4:12). This is not a word we can manipulate or spin to suit our whims. It is Jesus Christ, who comes with a fearsome power over all the elements, over life and death. "His eyes are like a flame of fire, and on his head are many diadems . . . He is clad in a robe dipped in blood, and the name by which he is called is The Word of God" (Rev 19:12-13).

He has come into our lives with that power, as our teacher, savior, brother, God. Let us welcome the Word of God, then, in the very words of God.

I.

What Is the Bible?

The Bible is the Word of God in human words. Because it comes to us from Almighty God, it has the power to be life-transforming. For God knows each of us, and he knows what we need when we open up the book.

Sometimes we find his Word thundering from above, sometimes whispering in a still, small voice, but always it is the Word sent by the All-Knowing, All-Loving, All-Powerful.

The Bible is a whole library of books written over the course of more than a thousand years, in many different styles, with many different points of view, by dozens of different writers.

But it is also one book, with one Author — God — telling one story: the heart-pounding, thrill-a-minute story of our salvation.

No other book has that kind of variety and unity, or unity-in-variety. It's what can make reading the Bible not just a pleasure, but one of the most exciting intellectual experiences of your life.

The story takes a long time to develop, and you'll meet many interesting characters along the way. By the end you'll realize that, from the very beginning, God always had a providential plan — a fatherly plan to save his children on earth. You'll also see how, like a master novelist, he sent people and events that foreshadowed later people and events, preparing his people for the greater things to come by giving them images that would help them understand.

Finally, there's one more thing that makes the Bible unique. You don't have to be satisfied with just reading it: you can step right into it. Wherever the sacraments are celebrated, they are the Bible in action. Reading the Bible helps prepare you for the sacraments, and in the sacraments everything you've read about comes to life right before your eyes.

Doesn't that sound like an adventure? Then let's get started.

2.

The Shape of the Bible

The Bible is a library of dozens of books. Like any good library, it has to be organized somehow, so that you can find the books you need.

Since the Bible starts with the beginning of time and ends with the end of time, you might expect the books to be arranged chronologically. Actually, the arrangement is both more complicated and more logical than that.

The two big divisions, of course, are the Old Testament and the New Testament. The Old Testament is all the books of Scripture written before the coming of Jesus Christ; the New Testament is all the books of Scripture written after the coming of Jesus Christ.

A more basic question is: What is a "Testament"? *Testament* is an English translation of the Greek word *diatheke*, which can more accurately be translated as "covenant." In the ancient world, a covenant was a solemn agreement that established a family bond between two parties — marriage and adoption, for example, were covenant relationships, as were international alliances. The Old Covenant and the New represent stages in God's relationship with his people.

In each of these two big divisions, the Old and the New, the books are arranged in groups according to type.

The Old Testament

There are four main divisions in the Old Testament:

1. The Law. These are the five books of Moses, the foundation of everything else in the Old Testament. They tell the story of how Israel began and give rules for life and worship.

2. History. These books tell the story of Israel in the Promised Land, from the conquest through the kingdom and the Exile to the successful rebellion of the Maccabees.

3. Wisdom. These books include reflection on the order of creation as well as moral instruction on personal virtue, family life, governance, and fear of the Lord.

4. Prophecy. The word of God: his judgment on the wicked and his promises of comfort to the afflicted.

The New Testament

When we look at the New Testament, we can see the same kind of four-part structure:

1. The Gospels (the Law). The foundation of everything else in the New Testament, telling how Jesus Christ brought the New Law by which Christians live.

2. The Acts of the Apostles (history). The founding and spread of the new kingdom — the Church.

3. Epistles (wisdom). Meditations on the meaning of Christian wisdom, and practical advice on living the Christian life.

4. The Revelation (prophecy). How the final judgment brings punishment to the wicked and comfort to the afflicted.

Just remembering those four big divisions in the two Testaments will be a great help in getting familiar with what's in the Bible. Once you know the broad organization, you'll be surprised how quickly you can find just about anything you're looking for.

Why Two Testaments?
But why are there two testaments in the first place? Why do we still care about the Old Testament when we have the New Testament?

The answer is that each testament is incomplete without the other. They are two elements of a single plan. St. Augustine said that the New Testament is hidden in the Old, and the Old Testament is revealed in the New. On the day of his resurrection, Jesus proclaimed that all the promises of the Old Testament had been fulfilled (Lk 24:25-27). Peter's sermon in Acts 2:14-36 is a good example of how the first Christians preached that message.

That means we can't really understand the fundamental Christian message without the Old Testament. The New Testament doesn't abolish or revoke the Old Testament: on the contrary, it fulfills and renews it.

When you start reading, you'll begin to notice an even closer relationship. Time after time, events in one testament will remind you of things that happened in the other. Christian theologians call it *typology*: the way earlier things foreshadow later things. For example, Christians see the binding of Isaac (Gen 22:1-19) as a foreshadowing, or "type," of the sacrifice of Jesus Christ on the Cross. That doesn't mean it was *only* a type: it was also a real event that happened to Abraham and Isaac. But God uses history, as a novelist would use his plot, to lead us on to a better understanding of his plan.

The *Catechism* says that typology represents a *dynamic* movement toward ultimate fulfillment (*CCC*, n. 130). Typology shows us the pattern in God's plan. Abraham's offering foreshadows the sacrifice of the Passover lamb during Israel's flight from Egypt (Ex 12) as well as the animal sacrifices of the Jerusalem Temple — which was built on the very spot where Abraham offered Isaac. Its ultimate fulfillment was in Christ's offering; but the Church continues to take part in that offering today, as we celebrate the Mass, the Eucharist of the "Lamb of God."

3.

Who Wrote the Bible?

God, of course, is the principal author of the Bible. He not only created the world and guided its events, but he also inspired the biblical account of that creation and history. God chose human authors to put divine things into human words, and he made use of their individual skills and styles and literary techniques. The human authors were true authors, but God acted in them and through them to reveal all that he wanted to reveal.

No one knows how many people wrote the Bible. Some books are entirely the work of one writer — Paul's letters, for example. Some, like Psalms or Proverbs, are compilations of works by many different authors, some of them named in the text. Some, like several of the historical books, were put together by an editor (or editors) who used various older sources; for example, the author of Kings often cites "the book of the chronicles of the kings of Israel."

Some of the letters in the New Testament tell us at the beginning who wrote them, and some of the prophets identify themselves as authors of their works. Many books of the Bible are anonymous. The books themselves don't identify the inspired authors, so we have to rely on tradition and scholarship. Tradition, for example, tells us that Moses wrote the five books of the Law and that the apostle John wrote Revelation.

Modern scholars often spend decades trying to figure out who wrote particular books. Did Moses really write the five books of the Law, or were they put together from four different documents, or were they compiled from oral traditions? Is the "John" who wrote Revelation really John the apostle, or some other Christian of the same name?

These are fascinating questions, but they are not as important to the average Bible reader as they are to scholars.

What we need to remember is that the books of the Bible as we have them are Scripture, inspired by God. The hypothetical sources of those books are not the Scriptures we rely on. It's good and useful to find out more about how a book was written. The more we find out, the better we can understand what it is saying. But we shouldn't forget that the Bible as we have it now is our inspired Scripture, not the Bible as we can theoretically reconstruct it.

Inspired by God

"All scripture is inspired by God and profitable for teaching, for reproof, for correction, and for training in righteousness" (2 Tim 3:16). But what do we mean when we say that these writings were "inspired by God"?

The Greek text of 2 Timothy says that "all" the Scriptures are "God-breathed." So inspiration means more than just God's help, approval, or agreement. It means God's authority, his authorship.

Catholic tradition speaks of "dual authorship" of the Bible. God is the "principal author," and the human writers are "instrumental authors." God's authority extends even to the human authors' word choices. They freely wrote only what God wanted them to write, and they wrote everything that God wanted them to write. They wrote the

Word of God in the very words of God, and yet they did this freely.

This is a great mystery — so great, in fact, that the Church compares the inspiration of Scripture to the incarnation of God the Son. In both cases, God acts as a true Father who stoops down to meet his children.

Through the incarnation, the eternal Word became flesh in order to share our life. Through inspiration, God accommodated his eternal word to human language.

Both the incarnate Word and the inspired Word are fully divine and fully human. In both, the human and the divine are inseparable. In both, the human is the instrument for communicating the divine.

Both inspiration and incarnation are divinely revealed mysteries, known only by faith, and otherwise unknowable by human means. Pope Pius XII said: "As the substantial Word of God became like men in all things, except sin, so the words of God, expressed in human language, are made like human speech in every respect, except error."

Scripture is indeed without error. An earlier

pope, Leo XIII, explained that inerrancy is a logical consequence of God's authorship. Inspiration, he said, "is essentially incompatible with error."

Still, "without error" does not adequately describe the Bible's authority. Other books can be free of mistakes — for example, a well-edited math textbook — but no other book has God as its author, and so no other text conveys God's saving power so purely. Jesus himself tells us: "The words that I have spoken to you are spirit and life" (Jn 6:63). Scripture is like a sacrament in the way it perfectly conveys the Word of God for the sake of our salvation.

4.

What Belongs in the Bible?

How do we know which books belong in the Bible?

It's a question we hear often today, when publishers parade any number of ancient texts before us as if they contained the long-suppressed truth about Jesus. The Gospel of Thomas, the Gospel of Judas, the Gospel of Philip — why aren't these books in our Christian Bible? Who decided what went in and what stayed out?

The Apostles entrusted the Scriptures to the Church as part of the deposit of faith — the sacred Tradition. Over time, guided by the Holy Spirit, the Church recognized the need to make a formal list of the writings that are divinely inspired. This complete list is called the "canon" of Scripture.

> *Canon* is the Greek word for "ruler" or "measuring stick."

At first, bishops produced such lists for the use of their local churches. Because there was no such thing as a printing press, most people — and even most churches — could not own a complete "Bible." Books were copied out laboriously by hand, so they were very expensive and somewhat rare, and private devotional reading was a luxury in which few Christians could indulge. Rather, believers heard the Scriptures proclaimed in the course of the Church's public worship — in the Mass. The oldest canons are simply lists of the books that could be read at Mass.

Bishops were sometimes motivated to draw up a canon because heretical groups were introducing strange "gospels" and attributing them to the early disciples of Jesus. An early bishop of Antioch, for example, publicly forbade the churches in his region to use a purported "Gospel of Peter" that was in circulation.

Many of these rejected texts have re-emerged in our own day, excavated by archeologists or historians. Scholars and churchmen call them "apocrypha," which is Greek for "hidden," since many of these texts were suppressed by the Church.

Though they are promoted breathlessly by the media, they are unreliable texts, produced at a much later date than the true Gospels — and though some of them are orthodox in their doctrine, most of them make for dull reading. There are very good reasons why they didn't make the Church's official canons of the Bible.

Several canonical lists have survived from the early centuries of the Church. St. Athanasius witnesses to the contents of the New Testament, exactly as we have them today, in A.D. 367. The bishops of the Church confirmed this canon at the local councils of Hippo (A.D. 393) and Carthage (397 and 419). The final canon was also ratified by the fourth-century Pope Damasus at a synod in Rome.

But, again, those official actions simply confirmed the long-established practice of the Church — the Tradition the Church had received from the Apostles.

The Old Testament

When Jesus and His disciples quoted "Scripture," they meant what we call the Old Testament —

the collection of sacred writings that made up the Bible of the Jews.

But how did the people of Israel decide which books were sacred and which were not? We can see in the Old Testament that there were several instances of "canonization" of Scripture, and they usually coincided with a renewal of God's covenant with his people.

Through Noah, God gave humanity a simple law to follow (Gen 9). Moses, in turn, recorded God's law and, in doing so, created a sort of "canon" (Ex 24:3-8).

The Second Book of Kings portrays the reformer Josiah as rediscovering the long-neglected book of the law and then proclaiming it publicly (2 Kings 23:2). Similarly, after returning from exile, the priest Ezra reintroduced the law to the people by reading it aloud in the assembly (Neh 8:3, 5-6).

Throughout their history, the people of Israel preserved the collection of sacred writings. In the three centuries before Christ, Jews in Egypt translated these into Greek, producing an edition known as the Septuagint (named in honor of the team of seventy translators, the *septuaginta,* sometimes abbreviated with the Roman numeral LXX. The contents of the Septuagint constitute one early canon, which was accepted by many Greek-speaking Jews throughout the world. In the New Testament writings, the Apostles appear to use the Septuagint, and so did the ancient Church Fathers.

By the time of Jesus, there was a general consensus as to which books belonged to Scripture — which books could be read in worship in the synagogues and the Temple. A few of the more recent books, though, were still debated. The books of Maccabees, for example, and some of the Wisdom books, were accepted by many Jews, and they appeared with the Septuagint. But later rabbis rejected them, and today those books are not in the Jewish Bible.

Catholics, following ancient tradition, accept those seven later books as part of the Old Testament. Almost all Protestant bodies follow the later Jewish tradition in rejecting them. The debated books are often called Deuterocanonical, from a Greek word meaning "second canon." For a Catholic, they are in no way less inspired than the

Protocanonical ("first-canon") books. They usually do not appear in Protestant Bibles, however. To a Catholic, therefore, a Protestant Bible is incomplete.

The New Testament

To the very first Christians, "Scripture" meant what we call the Old Testament. In the beginning, when Christianity was mostly centered in Jerusalem, there was no need to write much more than that. When the Apostles preached, they interpreted the law, the prophets, and other writings in light of the death, resurrection, and glorification of Jesus Christ. But in just a few years Christianity spread throughout Palestine, and then throughout the Roman Empire and beyond. Now it was impossible for the Apostles to be and teach everywhere at once.

Often, the Apostles would write to churches they had founded, giving them encouragement, settling disputes, and telling them what the true teaching of Christ was on certain questions that had come up. These letters, coming from Christ's chosen vicars, were read aloud when the congregation assembled to worship. These letters were the first Christian Scriptures — messages from the Apostles to congregations that they couldn't immediately visit in person.

For the same reasons, the Christian community began to need written accounts of Jesus' life. When most Christians were people who had actually met Jesus and seen the events of his ministry, there was no need for a book to tell them what they already knew. But soon the number of Christian converts who had never seen Jesus on earth far outweighed the number of original followers of Jesus. To be sure the true history of Jesus' ministry was being recited when they assembled for worship, Christians who had seen the events or had good information began to write down the stories in "Gospels" — stories of the Good News.

But only those letters that carried the authentic message of the Apostles, and only those Gospels that told the true history of Christ's life on earth, would be suitable for reading at Christian worship. And many more books were written than ended up in the New Testament: see Lk 1:1, where Luke tells us that many histories of Jesus' life had already been written by the time he picked up his pen.

Today, it seems like a hopeless task to sort out the hundreds of documents and decide which ones hold the authentic message. But it was not nearly so hopeless when the task was being done. The Church was already making its decisions while the Apostles were still alive. Jesus had been a popular preacher, and thousands of people had seen at least part of what he did. Peter, Paul, and many of the other Apostles had traveled extensively and spoken to thousands in their time. There were thousands of eyewitnesses in the Church who could verify firsthand what Christ and the Apostles said and did.

By the middle of the second century — when there were still people alive who had heard the Apostles preaching — the list of books was already taking shape. The Muratorian Canon, which was most likely written in the late 100s, lists the books of the New Testament almost as we list them today.

Later Church councils codified the Christian canons of both the Old Testament and the New. The Council of Trent authoritatively listed the books of the Scriptures, reacting to the Protestants who rejected the Deuterocanonical books. But the canon is not a late invention: it was a consensus reached very early, and the later councils only confirmed what had already been the teaching and practice of the Catholic Church.

5.

The Bible and the Church

The Bible is the founding document of the Church, and the Bible comes to life in the Church. Without the Church, in fact, you're missing half of the story.

Jesus wanted his revelation — the Gospel — to be transmitted in a reliable way through the ages. So Jesus commissioned the Apostles to pass on what he had revealed to them. We see in the Acts of the Apostles that they did this by preaching, teaching, praying, writing, and especially by their ritual actions (baptism in water, the breaking of the bread, the laying on of hands).

God revealed himself to the ages, then, through Scripture and Tradition, and both are safeguarded by the Church. The content of Scripture, the canon, was preserved through Tradition. The correct interpretation of Scripture also depended upon Tradition. St. Paul gave the Church instructions that we still follow today: "stand firm and hold to the traditions which you were taught by us, either by word of mouth or by letter" (2 Thess 2:15).

Scripture and Tradition are closely connected. They depend upon one another. They confirm one another, for they both come from the same source: God.

Tradition keeps us honest. All the generations of Christians who have gone before us are witnesses to the Apostles' way of interpreting the Bible. So we want to interpret the Bible as they did. A Catholic has the help of the whole Church in reading the Bible — the saints of the past and Christians of the present, from every corner of the globe. How's that for a privilege?

The Church interprets the Bible under the guidance of the Holy Spirit (see an illustration of this in Acts 8:29-35). Jesus Christ promised that he would always guide his Church. He gave his Apostles the authority and power to teach true doctrine, and the Apostles passed down that authority to their successors, in an unbroken line to the bishops of today. This teaching authority, called the magisterium, helps us interpret the Bible without wandering into error.

And the Spirit said to Philip, "Go up and join this chariot." So Philip ran to him, and heard him reading Isaiah the prophet, and asked, "Do you understand what you are reading?" And he said, "How can I, unless some one guides me?" And he invited Philip to come up and sit with him. Now the passage of the Scripture which he was reading was this:

"As a sheep led to the slaughter
Or a lamb before its shearer is silent,
So he opens not his mouth.
In his humiliation justice was denied him.
Who can describe his generation?
For his life is taken up from the earth."

And the eunuch said to Philip, "Please, about whom does the prophet say this, about himself or about some one else?" Then Philip opened his mouth, and beginning with this Scripture he told him the good news of Jesus.

—Acts 8:29-35

Jesus didn't leave his followers without guidance. He left them a Church, charged with preaching the Good News to everyone in the world and given the authority to do it right (see Mt 28:18-20).

Because the Church was given the authority to teach biblical doctrine reliably, you can always look to the Church when something in the Bible seems confusing. The Catechism of the Catholic Church, which has a superb index, is one good place to go looking for answers.

The Bible and the Liturgy

It's important to remember that the "canon" of the New Testament was primarily a list of books that were suitable for reading in the liturgy. The Muratorian Canon, for example, also lists *The Shepherd of Hermas* as a good book to read anywhere else — but specifies that it may not be read in worship. We tend to forget the place of the Bible in the liturgy, but in fact that's what "Scripture" means: the books that may be read in liturgy.

That doesn't mean it's wrong to read the Bible

outside the liturgy. Absolutely not! Read as much as you can, as often as you can. But the native environment of Scripture is the liturgy, because the liturgy is where Scripture comes to life — where the written text becomes a living Word. All the promises of the Old Testament and the New point toward the liturgy of the Church, which is an earthly sharing in the eternal liturgy in heaven.

Reading the Bible without participating in the liturgy is like reading a great adventure story and slamming the book shut before the final chapter. How does it all turn out? Does good triumph? Do the promises all come true? The Christian liturgy, especially the Mass, is the answer to all those questions.

At home, you can read the Bible — and that's wonderful. But when you go to Mass, you *live* the Bible.

6.

How to Understand the Bible

With the help of the Church, then, we're ready to open the Bible and read. But first, a little preparation.

The Bible Is Literature

Why do we need preparation to read the Bible? Can't we just open it up and read it?

Yes, we can, but we might not always understand what we're reading.

That's because the Bible is literature. That seems too obvious to need saying: of course, the Bible is literature — it's got words in it. But we have to understand that a lot of what we do automatically when we read any kind of literature is actually quite complex.

When we read a detective story, we know what the rules of the genre are, and — without thinking about it — we understand the story within those rules. They're different from the rules for a corporate annual report or a syndicated humor column, but we know what to expect from each of those, too.

In the detective story, we expect something plausible but not really true. In the annual report, we expect real facts dressed up to make the corporation look good. In the syndicated humor column, we expect exaggeration and distortion meant to make us laugh.

But what would happen if we had the wrong expectations? What would happen if we read the annual report expecting it to work like a syndicated humor column? We might enjoy it a lot more, but we certainly wouldn't get the message the writers meant us to get.

When we read something, we understand it completely only if we know what kind of literature we're reading. Most of the time we don't have to think about it: we've been reading the same sorts of things all our lives, so we just naturally know what to expect.

But that's not true when we approach the Bible. Scripture is many different kinds of literature, and unless we know which kind we're reading, we won't really understand what we're reading.

The problem is that most of us don't recognize the literary forms of three thousand years ago as easily as we recognize a detective story when we see it.

> ...although there are a couple of excellent detective stories in the book of Daniel!

Before we can understand what the writers of Scripture were trying to tell us, we have to know a little about the literary forms they used.

The Kinds of Literature

Some of the writing in the Bible tells a story. The book of Jonah is a good example. Like any good story, it has a plot (with a beginning, middle, and end), a hero you care about, and a good moral to be learned at the end of it. That doesn't mean the story can't be true, but the primary purpose of the book is to tell a good story that reveals a moral truth. Esther, Ruth, and Tobit are other examples of books where the main purpose is to tell that kind of story.

There's also straightforward history, where the

important thing is to have an accurate record of events. In the Bible, history is always told from a religious perspective, so the narration is never shy about making it clear when national disasters are the result of the sins of the people or their leaders. The books of Samuel and Kings are good examples of historical writing, as are the Gospels and Acts in the New Testament.

Prophecy brings God's word to his people to warn them of judgment or to promise them salvation. The book of Isaiah is a good example of prophecy.

Poetry expresses the deepest emotions of the poet — love, awe, despair, sorrow, and all the feelings poets have tried to express through the ages. The Psalms, for example, are poetry, and many of the prophets were also poets.

Wisdom literature conveys advice about living the good life in a way that appeals to any intelligent and philosophical person. The book of Proverbs is the best-known example of wisdom literature.

Letters, or "epistles," send encouragement or advice to specific people or groups. The letters of St. Paul in the New Testament are good examples:

some address whole congregations, while others (like Philemon) address individual friends.

Apocalypses describe, in figurative language, the end of time and the final judgment. The book of Revelation (also known as the Apocalypse) is the best-known example.

The Bible Is One Book

With all these different kinds of literature, written over so many centuries, the Bible is still one book. It tells the history of our salvation, which is certainly the most exciting story ever told.

One way of understanding this "salvation history" is by seeing the story as a series of covenants — sacred bonds between God and humanity. In the Bible, we read how God makes a covenant with Adam; then with Noah and his whole extended family; then with Abraham and his descendants, a whole tribe; then with Moses and the whole nation of Israel; then with David, a king and ruler of many nations; and finally the New Covenant, through Jesus Christ, which embraces all humanity.

Each of these covenants moves a little closer to

repairing the damage caused by our sin. Because we, God's creatures, constantly sin and reject God, God can only bring us back to a right relationship with him by slow and painful stages. The whole Bible is really the story of God leading his people back to him.

7.

Your Reading Program

Reading about the Bible is interesting and useful, but reading
the Bible itself is our goal. By now you have the
tools you need to open up the Bible and start
mining some of its riches.

But how do you go about it? What should you
read first, and how should you read it?

1. From Front to Back

Many people decide to read the whole Bible from
the beginning to the end, and that's a very good
goal. But it may be a hard one to stick to.

You already know by now that the Bible is
filled with all different kinds of literature. Some of
the stories in Genesis are absolutely riveting, so it's
easy to get started at the beginning. Exodus starts
out with stories that have provided the plot for
many action and adventure movies, so the first few
chapters just fly by,

But not everything in the Bible is that kind of

reading. Numbers, for example, has two complete censuses of the people of Israel, taken forty years apart. They are not riveting reading. They're not meant to be. The United States Census from 1870 isn't riveting reading, either. But if you're researching your family's genealogy, or trying to understand the demographic changes of the late nineteenth century, it's essential information.

Some parts of the Bible are meant for reference: like the census, they contain essential information, but even the original authors never expected that people would want to read them straight through.

The trouble for people who set out to read the Bible front to back usually comes when they hit the last chapters of Exodus, or nearly the whole book of Leviticus, where the social and ritual laws of Israel are given in exhaustive detail. Those laws were and still are essential information, but reading them straight through is hard — and unnecessary when you're just starting out. There'll be plenty of time later to refer back to those laws when you need to understand some of the customs that come up in the later stories. Then the laws will be much more interesting, because you'll actually be seeing how they worked in real life.

So, if you decide to read the Bible from beginning to end, don't be ashamed to skip ahead if you get bogged down. It's far better to read most of the Bible than to read a book and a half at the beginning and then put it down forever, afraid to open the book again.

2. Following the Lectionary

Another good way to read almost all the Bible is to follow the daily lectionary. Certain readings are assigned to be read at Mass every day. On Sundays and feast days, the readings are selected because they go together and illuminate each other. So following the lectionary can help you understand the readings in the whole context of salvation history. Typology comes to life: you see how things in the Old Testament foreshadowed the things in the New, and how the events of the whole Bible find fulfillment in the Church's sacraments.

Remember that the liturgy is Scripture's native environment. When you follow the lectionary, you're reading the Bible from the heart of the Church.

One of the advantages of reading along with the lectionary is that the homily at Mass will usually be based on one of the passages you've been reading. What better way to understand the Bible than to have the Church's clergy explain it to you as you go? You might even decide to start going to Mass every day, just so you can hear what the priest will have to say about what you've been reading. And going to Mass is itself a good thing. It's the way to see *mystagogy* at work — how the Scriptures unfold and reveal themselves in the liturgy.

Mystagogy is post-baptismal instruction in the divine mysteries of the Christian faith.
It discloses the truth hidden in the Scriptures and celebrated and fulfilled in the sacraments.
(See *Catechism of the Catholic Church,* 1075)

There are disadvantages, of course. You don't read whole books in sequence this way, and it can be hard to follow a long story that you read only in short segments. But there's no rule against reading more than the daily reading. If you want to understand the context, by all means, read the whole chapter. If you end up reading the whole book because you can't put it down (and that can certainly happen, because there are some real page-turners in the Bible), there's nothing wrong with that.

3. Reading Your Favorite Stories

Maybe you remember some favorite Bible stories from your childhood — stories that always fired your imagination and left you feeling excited and inspired. Why not go back and read those stories now?

At the end of this book is a section called "Where to Find . . ." All your favorite stories are there, and probably some you don't remember. It's a good place to start.

Many Bibles have references in the margin or bottom of the page that point you to revealing passages in other books of the Bible. Once you've read and enjoyed a story, follow some of those references. You might find the same story told from a different point of view. Or you might find a later writer's meditation on the story you've just read. Or you might find a passage in the Law that illuminates the customs described in the story, or a prophet's remarkable prediction of the events. And if you follow the references from that passage, who knows where you might end up? It's a great way to see how everything in the Bible is interrelated and interdependent.

Reading your favorite stories may not be the best way to read the whole Bible, but it's a great way to start reading and remembering what an adventure the Bible can be. Even if you never did more than that, you'd probably be way ahead of most Christians.

However you decide to read, keep at it. Set aside a time during the day for reading the Bible. Do you have ten minutes to spare before breakfast? Can you eat lunch ten minutes faster and leave a bit of time at the end? Do you have ten minutes to spare before you go to bed? Ten minutes is almost always enough time to read the day's readings from the lectionary, or one chapter from the book of your choice. You don't have to make it a big project. Just make it a little project — but one you stick with. You'll be surprised how such a small effort can make a huge difference in your faith.

8.

The Books of the Bible

Old Testament

The Pentateuch, or the Law

The first five books of the Bible were traditionally attributed to Moses. They include the story of the Beginnings of the world and of Israel as a nation, and they also provide the fundamental laws by which the Israelites were to live as a holy nation set apart for God.

Genesis means "beginning" in Greek: it tells the story of the beginning of everything. It starts with creation and ends with the ancestors of Israel moving to Egypt. In between we hear the stories of the Fall, the Flood, the Tower of Babel, Abraham, Isaac, Jacob, and Joseph, among many others.

Exodus, which means "going out," tells how the people of Israel escaped from slavery in Egypt and received the Law in the wilderness of Sinai. Their leader was Moses, whose own story takes up most of the early part of the book. The story of the ten plagues of Egypt, including the Passover, is in Exodus, and so are the Ten Commandments.

Leviticus is so named because it was a manual for the Levites. After Israel sinned by worshiping the Golden Calf, the Levites were set apart as the priestly tribe. Leviticus details the laws of ritual purity that the nation of Israel would have to follow to mark it as a holy nation belonging to God.

Numbers includes two censuses of the Israelites — thus the English name. The Hebrew name means "In the Wilderness," which is a good description of the rest of the book. It tells how Israel spent forty years wandering in the wilderness as punishment for the people's lack of faith in refusing to believe that the Lord would give Canaan into their hands.

Deuteronomy means "second law" in Greek. When the Israelites sinned yet again by worshiping pagan Moabite gods, it was clear that the people were not ready for the responsibility of being a holy nation. The law in Deuteronomy makes concessions to the people's "hardness of heart" — divorce, for example (see Deut 24:1, and compare how Jesus explains that law in Mt 19:3-9).

The Historical Books

These are the books that tell the history of Israel, from the conquest of the Promised Land through the years of the united kingdom and the divided kingdom, to the exile and the return of a remnant to rebuild destroyed Jerusalem.

Joshua tells how Israel conquered most of Canaan under Joshua, Moses' successor. The conquest goes well as long as Israel is faithful to the Lord's instructions; disobedience brings defeat. The famous story of the fall of Jericho is in Joshua.

Judges covers many years of turmoil in Israel, during which the Philistines and the remaining unconquered Canaanites constantly menaced the loosely confederated Israelite tribes. The book follows a pattern of apostasy, oppression, and redemption: Israel falls away from the worship of the True God, God allows Israel to fall into the hands of its enemies, and God sends a redeemer when Israel cries out for help. Many famous stories are in Joshua: Gideon's trumpet, Samson and Delilah, and Jephthah's daughter, to name a few.

Ruth is a beautiful romance that takes place in the time of the Judges. The Moabite widow Ruth follows her mother-in-law back to Israel: "For where you go I will go, and where you lodge I will lodge; your people shall be my people, and your God my God" (Ruth 1:16). Eventually, she marries the wealthy and virtuous Boaz, becoming the great-grandmother of King David, and thus one of the ancestors of Jesus Christ.

Samuel, which is divided into two books, tells the story of the beginning of the kingdom in Israel. When the people demand to have a king, God sends Samuel to anoint Saul as King of Israel. But Saul forfeits the kingdom by his disobedience, and God sends Samuel to anoint David instead. Much of 1 Samuel is taken up with the long struggle between the increasingly insane Saul and David, who refuses to take Saul's life even when he has the opportunity. Most of 2 Samuel is devoted to David's long reign. The story of David and Goliath is in 1 Sam 17; God's covenant with David, with his promise to give David an everlasting dynasty, is in 2 Sam 7.

Kings, which also is in two books, picks up the

story where 2 Samuel left off at the end of David's reign. 1 Kings tells of the glorious reign of Solomon, whose apostasy brings on the division of the kingdom after his death. Ten of the twelve tribes rebel and form the northern kingdom of Israel; only Judah and Benjamin are left to the house of David. Cycles of apostasy and reform end with destruction for both kingdoms, first Israel and then Judah. The northern tribes are scattered, never to return; the two southern tribes are exiled to Babylon.

Chronicles, also in two books, covers much of the same history as Samuel and Kings. The emphasis in Chronicles is more theological, and the author makes a special effort to show us David as the pattern of the ideal king.

Ezra tells how some of the people of Judah returned to their homeland after decades in exile. Under the leadership of Ezra the priest, they attempted to rebuild the Temple in Jerusalem and live their lives in obedience to the Law of Moses.

Nehemiah tells how Nehemiah, who had been cupbearer to the Persian king, returned to Jerusalem to lead the rebuilding. Much of it is from Nehemiah's own memoirs — a unique first-person narrative of ancient Jerusalem just after the Exile.

Tobit tells a story, set in the exiled Israelite community, of an Israelite whose attempt to keep his family on the path of righteousness receives unexpected help from a disguised angel. (Tobit is one of the deuterocanonical books.)

Judith is the heroic story of an Israelite woman who saves her people from conquest by the Assyrians. (Judith is one of the deuterocanonical books.)

Esther tells the story of an exiled Israelite woman who becomes Queen of Persia and saves her people from a genocidal conspiracy. (Some parts of Esther are deuterocanonical; the book is longer in Catholic Bibles than in Protestant or modern Jewish Bibles.)

1 Maccabees tells the history of the Jewish rebellion against the oppressive Seleucid emperors who tried to force paganism on the Jews, and how — against all odds — the rebellion succeeded. (1 Maccabees is one of the deuterocanonical books.)

2 Maccabees narrates some of the same events found in 1 Maccabees, emphasizing the witness of blood: martyrdom. (2 Maccabees is one of the deuterocanonical books. Some Bibles place the books of Maccabees at the end of the Old Testament, rather than here at the end of the historical books.)

The Wisdom Books

These are mostly poetic books. Some of them, like Psalms and the Song of Solomon, are pure poetry; others, like Proverbs and Wisdom, are collections of sage advice on how to live the good life; still others, like Job and Ecclesiastes, address life's most difficult questions. Wisdom literature has a broad appeal: it speaks to the concerns of all people, not just the Israelites, and uses those concerns to lead all people closer to God.

Job asks the most difficult question in all of philosophy: why do good people suffer? Job is prosperous and serves God faithfully. Satan, acting as prosecutor in God's court, predicts that Job will curse God if he loses all his blessings. So Job loses everything, but he still will not curse God. However, he also refuses to admit that his downfall was the result of his sin, even when his friends try to persuade him to confess his unknown sin and pray to God for forgiveness. In the end, God himself vindicates Job, but Job can never hope to understand the reasons for his suffering. The wisdom and power of God are infinite and unsearchable.

Psalms is the great hymn-book of Israel, full of liturgical poetry that still resounds in the words of our Mass today. Many of the Psalms are attributed to King David, who was the greatest poet of ancient Israel. There are Psalms for every occasion and every feeling, and many of them have a prophetic as well as poetic character. Psalm 22, for example, was quoted by Jesus on the Cross. (There are two different numbering systems for the Psalms. Most modern Bibles use the Hebrew numbering system, but some older Catholic Bibles use the system from the Septuagint, the Greek translation used by the Jews of the Dispersion.)

> My God, my God, why have
> you forsaken me?
> — Ps 22:1

Proverbs is a collection of wise sayings. Many are attributed to Solomon, whose wisdom was legendary, but others come from other sources. Some passages closely resemble wisdom literature from other cultures of the Near East, suggesting that Hebrew wisdom literature could have a broad appeal to other nations as well.

Ecclesiastes asks the most basic existential question: Is life worth living? "All is vanity," says the author, and nothing in life seems worthwhile. But the book ends by concluding that fearing God and keeping his commandments are the things that make life worth living.

The Song of Solomon, or the **Song of Songs**, is a love poem that celebrates the mutual delight of a bride and bridegroom. But Jewish and Christian theologians have always seen a deeper meaning as well: an allegory of the love of God for his people.

The Wisdom of Solomon celebrates Wisdom personified, and tells the story of salvation history as guided by Wisdom. (Wisdom is one of the deuterocanonical books.)

Sirach (or the Wisdom of Jesus, son of Sirach, also known as Ecclesiasticus) is a collection of wisdom on the subject living life well. It specifically emphasizes the importance of wisdom in family life.

The Prophets

Prophets brought God's word to people who needed to hear it — sometimes a word of judgment to the smug and complacent, sometimes a word of comfort to the oppressed and afflicted. The prophetic books in the Bible are divided into "major" and "minor" prophets according to the length of the books — not because some were more important than others.

The Major Prophets

Isaiah includes prophecies from a long period before and during the Exile. Isaiah foretells judgment on Judah for its sins, but also brings the comforting promise that a faithful remnant will return to Jerusalem, and ultimately the Lord's Anointed — the Messiah — will come to save all God's people.

Jeremiah prophesied during the tragic period just before and just after the Babylonian destruction of Jerusalem. His book is the longest in the Bible, and it includes some dramatic stories of his confrontations with wicked kings and ministers, as well as his famous oracles. Like Isaiah, Jeremiah foretold destruction for Judah, but he also promised a time when God would institute a New Covenant with his people, and all their tears would be wiped away.

Lamentations is a series of poems, attributed to Jeremiah, on the destruction of Jerusalem. Although the poems are filled with sadness, they are also filled with faith that, even in disaster, God will not abandon his people.

Baruch is attributed to Jeremiah's secretary. It brings a message of consolation to captive Israelites everywhere: Jerusalem will not abandon them, and the way of Moses is still best and wisest. (Baruch is one of the deuterocanonical books.)

Ezekiel is full of strange imagery and hard sayings. The prophet himself was called while in exile in Babylon; he sees visions of the heavenly worship, and he looks forward to a perfected Israel after the Exile, where the liturgy of the Temple will be perfectly celebrated.

Daniel is a combination of prophecy and inspiring stories. Much of the book is taken up with an apocalyptic vision of the coming of the Son of Man. The famous stories of Daniel in the lions' den and the three young men in the furnace are also in Daniel. Some sections of Daniel are deuterocanonical, including the famous "detective stories" in which Daniel's wisdom saves Susanna from the elders and exposes the deceit of the priests of Bel.

The Minor Prophets

Hosea compares Israel to an adulterous wife, but promises that God will redeem his people even after their adultery.

Joel is a vision of impending judgment (the "Day of the Lord"), a call to repentance, and a promise of the sending of the Holy Spirit.

Amos pronounces judgment against Israel's enemies, but the most terrible judgment against Israel itself for the people's infidelity. But in the end the house of David will be restored.

Obadiah pronounces judgment against Edom, traditional enemy of Israel.

Jonah tells the sometimes comic story of a reluctant prophet who tries to run away when God sends him to preach judgment to the hated Ninevites. Of course, he can't run away from God, and much to his disgust, the Ninevites repent and are spared. God is merciful even to the enemies of Israel if they repent.

Micah chastises the leaders of Judah for bringing on God's judgment, but promises that a Prince of Peace will come from the town of Bethlehem.

Nahum rejoices in the coming destruction of Nineveh, the cruel destroyer of nations, but warns Jerusalem to expect the same fate for her infidelity.

Habakkuk paints the advancing Babylonians as God's instruments for chastising Judah, but promises that Israel will not be entirely destroyed.

Zephaniah describes the Day of the Lord, when terrible judgment will come to the wicked, but the righteous will finally be freed from their affliction.

Haggai prophesied after the return from the Exile, urging the people to push forward with the stalled rebuilding of the Temple.

Zechariah prophesied to shake the returned exiles out of their complacency. He promised them that a king and savior would come to them, riding humbly on a donkey.

Malachi chastises the chosen people for hypocrisy, but foresees a time when every nation will offer God a pure sacrifice.

New Testament
The Gospels

The Gospels tell the story of Jesus' life and ministry. Each of the four different authors picks different details to emphasize, but they all have the same story to tell. Matthew, Mark, and Luke are often known as the "Synoptic" Gospels, because they tell many of the same stories in the same way. John seems to have been written later and tells the same story from a different point of view.

Matthew was probably written for Jewish Christians in Palestine. It portrays Jesus as the "son of Abraham" (Mt 1:1), who fulfills the covenant of Abraham; it portrays him as a New Moses, the giver of the new Law; and as the Son of David, the true king. Matthew includes the famous Sermon on the Mount (chapters 5-7).

> The book of the genealogy of Jesus Christ, the
> son of David, the son of Abraham.
> — Mt 1:1

Mark is attributed to John Mark, a disciple of Peter. Mark wrote down the story of Jesus as Peter had proclaimed it. He emphasizes Jesus' divine sonship and status as God's anointed, an identity proved by his miracles, but kept secret from those who would misunderstand him as a mere earthly king.

Luke, the only non-Jew among the Gospel writers, was a companion of Paul. Like Paul, he emphasizes that Christ came to save all Israel and the Gentiles. He wrote for a Gentile audience, carefully explaining Jewish customs. He also added the story of Jesus' conception and birth, which he may have heard from Mary herself.

John emphasizes the heavenly identity of Jesus and provides more expansive theological reflection. It places the events of Jesus' life in the context of Jewish festivals, which Christ fulfilled. John emphasizes the Christian sacraments, especially baptism and Eucharist. He depicts Jesus' miracles as "signs" that point to deeper mysteries.

The Acts of the Apostles

The Acts of the Apostles, written as a sequel to Luke's Gospel, tells how the early Church grew from a handful of believers in Jerusalem to many thousands throughout the world. It concentrates on the work of Peter and Paul and emphasizes the mission of the Holy Spirit in the life of the Church.

The Epistles

These are letters from the Apostles to congregations that needed encouragement, discipline, or advice. By far the largest number bear Paul's name.

Epistles of Paul

Romans, the longest of Paul's letters, is a profound theological study of salvation in Christ. Paul demonstrates that both Jews and Gentiles are sinful and stand in need of a savior, and he traces their predicament back to the original sin of Adam. The Church shows forth God's plan to save "all Israel" and the Gentiles (Rom 11:26-27).

1 Corinthians gives Paul's fatherly advice for order, both in the Church and in private moral life.

He describes the Church as the Body of Christ and Christians as Temples of the Holy Spirit. He discusses the variety of God's gifts and vocations, married and celibate. He is concerned with proper doctrine and observance of the sacraments.

2 Corinthians defends Paul's ministry after a difficult time with the Corinthian Church. Paul speaks more personally here than he usually does. He is concerned that "false apostles" have misled the Christians of Corinth.

Galatians defends the orthodox understanding of the Gospel against those who would subject Gentile Christians to circumcision and other ceremonial laws of the Old Covenant. It is a passionate plea for Christians to recognize that the cross of Christ fulfilled the Old Covenant and inaugurated a "new creation" (Gal 6:15) and renewed Israel (6:16).

Ephesians teaches new Christians about the "mystery" of Christ and the Church. Christ reigns in heaven (Eph 1:20) and renews the world through his Church (3:10). Paul speaks of the Church as the body and bride of Christ (5:22-32) and as a Temple of the Holy Spirit (2:21-22).

Philippians was written to express Paul's gratitude for the generosity of the Christians of Philippi. It is an affectionate letter, though it also challenges the Philippians to continue their growth in maturity. Paul warns against false teachers.

Colossians addresses new Christians who have been misled by false teachers. The letter emphasizes the supremacy of Christ as creator and redeemer and the saving power of baptism.

1 Thessalonians is an encouraging letter to new Christians who were already facing persecution and other pressures. Paul writes at some length about the last things, death and judgment, and he reassures the Thessalonians that their dead will be raised, and that the coming judgment will be vindication for Christians.

2 Thessalonians reinforces the themes of 1 Thessalonians, clarifying teaching on Christ's return, and exhorting Christians to live orderly, normal lives of diligent work. He reminds them to hold fast to what they have been taught, either by writing or orally.

1 and 2 Timothy contain advice and instructions to a young bishop — his personal conduct, doctrine, public worship, and the discipline of his congregation.

Titus, like the letters to Timothy, advises a young bishop on private and public conduct.

Philemon is a personal note begging one of Paul's friends to take back his runaway slave, Onesimus, without punishing him. By using family language (father, son, brother), Paul emphasizes the new bond that unites all Christians.

Other Epistles

Hebrews is an essay on salvation history and the theology of the covenant, very similar to the thought of St. Paul. Focusing especially on the priesthood, it shows how the institutions of the Old Covenant foreshadowed their greater fulfillment in Jesus Christ.

James emphasizes the importance of good works as the fruit of faith in Christ.

1 and 2 Peter give advice to Christians on how to live their lives amid temptations and persecutions.

1, 2, and 3 John were written to warn against specific false doctrines that were poisoning the community, and to encourage Christians to stay faithful to the true doctrine even when the false doctrine seems to be powerful.

Jude is an urgent warning against false doctrine, with examples of Old Testament figures who led people astray and suffered righteous judgment.

Revelation

Revelation, also called the **Apocalypse** (Greek for "unveiling"), is a series of visions of God's action in all of history and creation. Its narrative is symbolic, speaking of events and actions in terms of spiritual warfare and ritual worship — a heavenly liturgy, with altar, priests, vestments, hymns, chalices, and sacrifice. Through the mediation of angels, God reveals to the author, John, that the saints are already victorious and now the forces of evil will be defeated. Finally, the author sees a new heaven and a new earth, free from the pain and sin that plagued the old world, where God himself is the light and the temple. Though Revelation has a reputation for being filled with terrifying visions of war and catastrophe, it is really a message of profound consolation. Terrible judgments come to the wicked, but not one of God's faithful servants is lost.

9.

Where to Find ...

Many stories and doctrines appear in several different places in the Bible, but you can start with the references given here. For more complete (but still handy) references, Patrick Madrid's *Where Is* That *in the Bible?* and *Why Is* That *in Tradition?* are recommended.

Stories of the World's Beginning

Creation:	Gen 1:1-2:3
The creation of woman:	Gen 2:18-25
The Fall (the serpent in the Garden of Eden):	
	Gen 3
First promise of the Savior:	Gen 3:15
Cain and Abel:	Gen 4
Noah and the Flood:	Gen 6-9
The Tower of Babel:	Gen 11:1-9

Stories of the Patriarchs

The call of Abraham:	Gen 12:1-9
Abraham promised a child:	Gen 15:1-6
Abraham to be a father of nations:	Gen 17:1-21

Abraham bargains with God:	Gen 18:22-33
Sodom and Gomorrah:	Gen 19:1-29
The binding of Isaac:	Gen 22:1-19
Jacob takes Esau's blessing:	Gen 25:29-34
	Gen 27:1-45
Jacob's ladder:	Gen 28:10-17
Jacob marries Rachel:	Gen 29:9-30
Jacob wrestles with the angel:	Gen 32:22-32
Joseph sold into slavery:	Gen 37
Joseph and Potiphar's wife:	Gen 39
Joseph interprets Pharaoh's dream:	Gen 41
Joseph reconciles with his brothers:	Gen 45
Jacob brings his family to Egypt:	Gen 46

Stories of Moses and the Exodus

Moses in the bulrushes:	Ex 2:-11
The burning bush:	Ex 3:1-4:17
The ten plagues:	Ex 5-12
The Passover:	Ex 12:1-36
The parting of the Red Sea:	Ex 14
Manna from heaven:	Ex 16
Water from the rock:	Ex 17:1-8
	Num 20:2-13
The Ten Commandments given at Mt. Sinai:	
	Ex 19:16-- 20:20
	Deut 5:1-27
The Golden Calf:	Ex 32:1-14
Spies sent to Canaan:	Num 13:1- 14:38

Balaam's talking donkey:	Num 22:21-35
Death of Moses:	Deut 34

Stories of the Conquest and the Judges

Rahab hides the spies:	Josh 2
Capture of Jericho:	Josh 6
The sun stands still for Joshua:	Josh 10:12-14
Deborah and Barak:	Judg 4-5
Gideon's trumpet:	Judg 6
Samson and Delilah:	Judg 16
Ruth follows her mother-in-law:	Ruth 1

Stories of the United Kingdom

Call of Samuel:	1 Sam 3
Samuel anoints Saul:	1 Sam 8-9
Samuel anoints David:	1 Sam 16:1-13
David plays the lyre for Saul:	1 Sam 16:14-23
David and Goliath:	1 Sam 17
David conquers Jerusalem:	2 Sam 5:6-10
God's promise to the house of David:	2 Sam 7:5-16
David and Bathsheba:	2 Sam 11
Death of Absalom:	2 Sam 18
Solomon prays for wisdom:	1 Kings 3
Solomon and the Queen of Sheba:	1 Kings 10:1-13
Apostasy of Solomon:	1 Kings 11:1-13

Stories of the Divided Kingdoms

Israel rebels:	1 Kings 12:1-20
Elijah raises the widow's son:	1 Kings 17:17-24
Elijah and the prophets of Baal:	2 Kings 18:17-46
Elijah taken up into heaven:	2 Kings 2:1-12
Israel conquered and exiled:	2 Kings 17:1-18
Judith kills Holofernes:	Jud 13
Nebuchadnezzar destroys Jerusalem, carries its people to Babylon:	2 Kings 25

Stories of the Exile and After

The three young men in the furnace:	Dan 3
The writing on the wall:	Dan 5
Daniel in the lions' den:	Dan 6:6-24
Temple rebuilding begun:	Ezra 3
Beginning of the Maccabees' rebellion:	1 Mac 2:1-29
Judas purifies the Temple:	1 Mac 4:36-59
Martyrdom of the seven brothers:	2 Mac 7

Prophecies of Christ

The woman's seed will defeat the serpent:	Gen 3:15
A prophet like Moses:	Deut 18:15
A virgin gives birth to a king:	Is 7:14
The Suffering Servant:	Is 52:13 - 53:12
The New Covenant:	Jer 31:31-34

The divine/Davidic Shepherd: Ezek 34:11-31

The Son of Man: Dan 7:13-14

A king and savior enters Jerusalem, riding on a donkey:
      Zech 9:9

The institution of the Eucharist as a perpetual sacrifice
    among the nations: Mal 1:11

Jesus' Life
The Mysteries of the Rosary

Joyful Mysteries

The Annunciation: Lk 1:26-38

The Visitation: Lk 1:39-56

The Nativity: Lk 2:1-20

The Presentation: Lk 2:22-40

The Finding of the Child Jesus: Lk 2:41-51

Luminous Mysteries

Jesus' Baptism: Mt 3:13-17

The Wedding Feast at Cana: Jn 2:1-12

Proclamation of the Kingdom: Mt 4:17

The Transfiguration: Mt 17:1-8

The Institution of the Eucharist: Lk 22:14-20

Sorrowful Mysteries

The Agony in the Garden: Lk 22:39-53

The Scourging: Mt 27:24-26

The Crowning with Thorns: Mt 27:11-27

Carrying the Cross: Lk 23:26-32

The Crucifixion: Jn 19:18-42

Glorious Mysteries

The Resurrection:	Lk 24:1-53
The Ascension:	Lk 24:50-53
	Acts 1:9-11
The Descent of the Holy Spirit:	Acts 2:1-21
The Assumption of Mary:	Rev. 11:19-12:17
The Coronation of Mary:	Rev 12:1

Other Events in Jesus' Life

(Many of these stories are in more than one Gospel, but you can start with the references given here.)

Visit of the Wise Men:	Mt 2:1-12
Temptation in the desert:	Mt 4:1-11
The Sermon on the Mount	Mt 5-7
Raises Lazarus from the dead:	Jn 11:1-44
Palm Sunday:	Lk 19:29-40
Judas betrays Jesus:	Lk 22:47-53
Peter denies Jesus:	Jn 18:15-27
The road to Emmaus:	Lk 24:13-35
Doubting Thomas:	Jn 20:24-29

Jesus' Parables

Seven kingdom parables:	Mt 13:1-52
The workers in the vineyard:	Mt 20:1-16
The two sons:	Mt 21:28-32
The wicked tenants:	Mt 21:33-46
The marriage feast:	Mt. 21:1-14
The ten virgins:	Mt 25:1-13
The talents:	Mt. 25:14-30

The lost sheep:	Lk 15:1-7
The good Samaritan:	Lk 10:30-37
The prodigal son:	Lk 15:11-32
The widow and the judge:	Lk 18:1-8

The Birth of the Church

"I will build my Church":	Mt 16:17-19
The giving of the Holy Spirit:	Jn 20:22-23
Characteristics of the early Church:	Acts 2:42
Ordination of the first deacons:	Acts 6:5-6
Stephen, the first martyr:	Acts 6:8-8:1
Conversion of Saul (Paul):	Acts 9:1-19
Gentiles welcomed:	Acts 10:9-48
The Apostolic Council of Jerusalem:	Acts 15:1-29
Paul's missionary journeys:	Acts 13 ff

The Sacraments

Baptism:	Jn 3:5
	Mt 28:19
Holy Eucharist:	Lk 22:14-30
	1 Cor 10:15-17
	11:17-29
Confirmation:	Acts 8:14-17
Penance:	Mt 18:18
	Jn 20:19-23
	Jas 5:14-16
Matrimony:	Eph 5:21-33
Holy Orders:	Lk 22:19
	1 Tim 3:1-7
	1 Tim 4:14
Anointing of the Sick:	Jas 5:14-16

The Bible in the Mass

Trinitarian blessing :	Mt 28:19
Sign of the Cross:	Rev 7:3; prefigured in Ezek 9:4
"Amen":	1 Chron 16:36b
Apostolic greeting:	2 Cor 13:14
"The Lord be with you":	2 Thess 3:1
"I confess . . .":	After Ps 51; Jas 5:16; and others
"Lord, have mercy (*Kyrie*)":	Mt 17:15
Gloria:	Lk 2:14; Revelation (many texts)
First reading:	Usually, Old Testament
Responsorial psalm:	A psalm or biblical canticle
Second reading:	Usually, New Testament (but not the gospels)
"Alleluia":	Rev 19:1-6
Gospel:	From the Gospels
Altar:	Rev 6:9
Priestly vestments:	Rev 1:13, 4:4, 6:11

"Lift up your hearts":	Lam 3:41
"Holy, holy, holy" (*Sanctus*):	Rev 4:8
	Is 6:3
Eucharistic prayer:	1 Cor 11:23-26
The Great "Amen":	Rev 5:14
The Lord's Prayer:	Mt 6:9-13
Sign of Peace:	Jn 14:27
	Jn 20:19
"Lamb of God":	Jn 1:29
"Behold the Lamb":	Rev 19:9
"Lord, I am not worthy . . .":	Mt 8:8
Dismissal:	Lk 7:50
"Thanks be to God":	2 Cor 9:15
Consecrated celibates:	Rev 14:3-4

Some Famous Sayings

The Ten Commandments:	Ex 20
"The Lord bless you and keep you":	Num 6:24
"You shall love the Lord your God with all your heart, and with all your soul, and with all your might":	
	Deut 6:5
"The Lord is my shepherd":	Psalm 23:1
The Golden Rule:	Mt 7:12
"My soul magnifies the Lord" (the *Magnificat*):	
	Lk 1:46-55
"For God so loved the world":	Jn 3:16
"I am the bread of life":	Jn 6:35
"You have the words of eternal life":	Jn 6:68